IN DEFENSE OF THE

EIGHTIES

Riya Aarini

ISBN: 978-1-956496-13-0 (Paperback)

ISBN: 978-1-956496-14-7 (eBook)

Library of Congress Control Number: 2022923158

First published in Austin, Texas, USA

Visit www.riyapresents.com

CONTENTS

CONTENTS

ON HAIRSPRAY

If any word in the English language expressly
defines the decade of excess, it's *hairspray*. Hair was
deliberately teased a quarter-mile high, if not higher,
then generously sprayed to hold every strand perfectly
in place for the next six and a half hours—the exact
duration of a junior high school day. Touch-ups of the
indispensable toiletry were necessary at midday, but
in general, the relentless power of eighties hairspray
meant you couldn't bulldoze high-rise bangs, even
if you tried. Just revisit any one of the decade's glam
rock music videos to gauge the staying power of
eighties hairspray: playful tumbles with an ultra-neon-

pink electric guitar strapped across the shoulder, acrobatic leaps from the top of a stage showered with multicolored laser light beams, and even hours of perspiration couldn't knock down hair standing unfalteringly eight inches high. The copious use of hairspray wasn't limited to the entertainment world either. Students had a ball liberally spraying the sticky gunk, which wafted perilously into the lowest parts of the earth's stratosphere, causing the formation of ground-level ozone. Hairspray was so essential in this decade, that recognizing the eighties could be done immediately upon glancing at instant color photos showing youth flaunting hairstyles that defied gravity itself. At its lowest point, the superfluous volumes of hairspray applied during this decade contributed to today's global warming catastrophe. At its highest point, the admirable stamina of hairspray bafflingly glamourized an entire generation.

ON FREEDOM

Unlike today's overparenting that resembles totalitarian regimes, eighties moms and dads were reasonably laid-back. Parents rarely asked about where their kids spent entire stretches from mornings until late afternoons. You could explore five-acre fields, fish in the streams, and ride your bike home with a stinky trout in tow without Mom or Dad demanding to know where you'd been the last seven hours. And the trout would be immediately pan-fried and devoured without parents worrying about mercury contaminating the catch. Childhood in the eighties was largely self-directed, without constant meddling by adults, making it carefree and happy. Eighties kids reveled in the freedom to think, do, and say as they pleased without concerns of being suffocated under the confines of overprotection or being forced to pursue an ambitious academic, sports, or musical course. Kids naturally gravitated toward physical activities, which kept them occupied. Most youth joyfully rode bikes or skateboards down the neighborhood streets—even occasional falls and bruises didn't strike paralyzing fear into eighties parents like they would today. The active lifestyle of the eighties contrasted sharply with the current generation, where kids sit engrossed in tablets, smartphones, or high-tech gaming systems in unhealthy, sedentary ways. Parents in the decade of mellow unrestraint provided their kids with all of life's practical essentials: food, clothing, and a warm place to sleep. Along with these necessities was an abundance of freedom. Children experienced blissful growth without parents constantly hovering over their daily existence like mosquitoes preparing to take precise aim at a tender swath of skin. The precious gift of autonomy allowed eighties kids to become resilient and independent—qualities that are now as unfortunately rare as the endangered Madagascar banana.

ON PRE-GOOGLE

While information is useful, when excessive or incorrect, it can lead to disaster. Today's world struggles to stay afloat under a deluge of facts, with some worth knowing and others that should be skillfully avoided for the sheer sake of survival. Consider, for instance, the wealth of health information available to anyone with access to an online search engine. A person feeling slightly ill, perhaps with a fever and a mild cough, might search Google for a diagnosis instead of waiting for a doctor's appointment to open up one week later. After all, why live with an annoying cough and slight fever for seven more days when treatments are available to return you to instant, ruddy health? But after browsing the plethora of health articles online, this mildly feverish individual pieces together a wide array of symptoms, gives himself a misdiagnosis, and walks away convinced that he's developed in incurable disease that will cause him to die within the next five days. Panic ensues, and his discomfort quadruples. He calls everyone in his contacts list to let them know of his fatal condition, even going so far as to make funeral arrangements with dramatic eighties rock ballads being his funerary music of choice. Common as this scenario is these days, this type of foible just didn't happen in the eighties. Google wasn't invented, and a person in the eighties who felt somewhat ill was compelled to wait to visit the doctor, who'd provide him with an accurate diagnosis and a helpful course of treatment, thereby circumventing the possibility of catastrophizing to the point of death. Straightforward, plain, and simple—three words that unerringly summarize this glorious decade of less information.

ON COLLOQUIALISMS

The eighties were breezy and easy, and the colloquialisms of the day reflected that ease. Why bother going through the effort of greeting someone with a two-syllable word when you can get by with one? "Yo!" was preferred over "hello" or "good afternoon" by most of the carefree youth. Just the same, the casual "outta here" was far more favorable when parting with company than the formal and serious "goodbye" or the unnecessarily elongated phrase "see you later." Amazement, too, was expressed in unique verbal fashion. Upon feeling pleasantly surprised, an eighties youth would exclaim "far out" or "tubular" or even "radical," with the abbreviated form "rad" being just as commonplace and effective. Addressing another was also done uniquely. Punctuated somewhere in every statement was the informal "dude," as in "Awesome, dude!" or "Yo, dude, I'm here." And "dude" was usefully gender neutral, equally addressing a familiar male or female acquaintance or a friend or, on occasion, a stranger. We mustn't forget the valley influence. Eighties youth inundated their speech patterns with "like" as in "Like, yeah, totally" or "Like, no way." Rather than find yourself speechless at the popular expressions of the day, just chill, because the eighties were, like, one tubular decade, dude.

ON MUSIC

Hair bands, glamorized with the glossy orange lipstick, neon-purple eye shadow, and frantically teased hair that unabashedly competed with the prettiest fans of their day, ruled the rock music scene during this nostalgic decade. No one growing up listening to eighties music could forget that the hair bands rocked some of the most memorable music ever. Today's fans even go so far as to overlook their flaws, whether that was recklessly entertaining scores of overenthusiastic groupies in two-star hotel rooms or injecting themselves with toxic substances that would have left them far higher than the ratings on their manager's choice of hotel. Regardless of their outrageous, over-the-top lifestyle, the decade's charismatic front men made a show of their undeniable "it" factor. Insanely skillful electric guitarists produced sounds as heavenly as the taste of ambrosia. Soulful keyboardists could command the twinkle of stars if they wanted to. And ostentatious drummers performed nearly as impressively as the front men themselves. Together, they managed to produce a musical fusion of rock and pop, one that today's loyal fans continue to harken back to, longing for those uninhibited times of yesteryear. While glam rock was one fabulous choice of eighties music, teen pop idols also dominated the decade's charts. Pop stars' desperate, cheesy lyrics and puppy dog eyes that looked barely halfway into the depths of your soul enamored youngsters in their quest to feel understood. Nothing much has changed lyrically in today's pop music, as the romantic desperation and helplessness continue, but the flamboyancy of eighties artists gave them a special, enduring place in our hearts and music memory. And despite hair bands ruling the decade with all the mighty staying power of eighties hairspray, we'll never see the likes of them in their heyday again.

ON THE MULLET

Long known as the hairstyle that was strictly business up front with an uncontrollable party in the back, the eighties mullet took down conventional hairstyles like an unpopular heavyweight wrestled down a likable lightweight in an unfair match in the squared circle of the wrestling ring. The odds of gaining social approval by sporting a mullet were few, yet nevertheless possible. And this glimmer of hope ruled men's choice of hairstyle for an entire wasteful decade. Whether intentional, as in rock stars of the day, or unintentional, as in our most modest founding father Ben Franklin, relying on the mullet look fell into ill repute in later years. Men once proud to wear the mullet during the height of the eighties' experiments in hair fashion grew unsurprisingly discontented, even going so far as to regret their hairstyle of choice by the time the decade ended and common sense regained control over their everyday decisions. Despite unavoidably lending itself to ridicule, the mullet has astoundingly reemerged from its rightful resting place and sprung back into today's youthful hair trends. Combining extremes of both formal and informal characteristics, the mullet has successfully found its way into offices, warehouses, and other places of professional and semiprofessional work that do not enforce a strict dress code that prevents the party in the back from being approved. As highly debatable as the tackiness of mullets is, one thing is clear: the cut has made a contribution to the style choices for today's daring youth who show no fear in wearing a fluctuating trend that, at its worst, has the likelihood of appearing as unflattering as the mountainous silver pheasant that could have, in all actuality, spurred the eighties' mighty mullet craze.

ON ROLLING UP YOUR JEANS

No one knows why youth in the eighties committed to folding up the legs of their jeans. Looking back, it made no practical sense. But the strange fashion of rolling up the ankles of jeans two or three times, then folding the baggy legs into neat pleats and tucking them in was followed by legions of junior high kids in this decade of inexplicable fashion. Jeans were manufactured to hang at a certain length—wasn't that what correct sizing was for? Yet the youth of this era insisted on wearing their jean legs a bit higher. Even perfectly fitted jeans were modified by folding. The skinny, tapered leg look was one of junior high fashion par excellence. It was a trend that took off in the eighties, then crashed in the following decade, when its opposite—flared jeans—took over. Today's fashion gurus have reverted back to rolling up and tucking in the legs of jeans, even of those that fit exquisitely well in the first place. In contemporary times, it's definitely no longer a passing trend in jeans but rather here to stay. And it's all thanks to the decade of glam.

ON SHOULDER PADS

The surge of working women in the eighties ushered in the desire to express new confidence, power, and influence in a male-dominated sphere. Somehow, somewhere, one of the brightest bulbs on the colorful string of lights came up with the perplexing idea to convey the profound wealth and growing authority among female politicians, actresses, and ordinary professionals through the most unthinkable of avenues: the shoulder pad. Women strutting around society in shoulder pads extending an impressive eight inches across either shoulder assumed the intimidating look of helmeted defensive linebackers ready to tackle the oncoming quarterback in a game of American football. And that was their explicit intention. The predominance of the gigantic fabric-covered foam sewn into all styles of dresses and suits defeminized eighties women, magically putting them on par with eighties men in their sleek power suits and ties. Giant shoulder pads alone weren't enough to empower women of the eighties. Savvy females doubled their threat by coupling massive shoulder pads with enormously big hair.

Looks ruled everything in this fab decade, and females modified them with ridiculous precision. All it took was the exaggeration of simple shoulder pads—of all possible things that could be convincingly exaggerated—to give women of the eighties a look that was strikingly larger than life.

ON MIXTAPES

Long before streaming and digital playlists, customized eighties mixtapes conquered the music scene of youth culture. While mixtapes delivered immense auditory pleasure to the amateur listener, they required a great deal of work to create. Homemade mixtapes started with blank tapes that were used to record music scintillating to the ear. This was a herculean task, however, as it was necessary to listen to the radio for hours at a time, waiting on high alert for favorite songs to play—which never occurred in sequence but rather unpredictably—then immediately hitting record. The process to produce the perfect mixtape could take hours. Naturally, as a result of the hard work, the mesh of favorite music collected in one controllable medium was incredibly satisfying. Swapping mixtapes with friends was a fun pastime too. Mixtapes also served as links between the amorously inclined. Giving a mixtape consisting of ten carefully selected music tracks to a love interest was a tender way to show affection and trust, no matter how painfully shy was the individual. Of course, being homemade, mixtapes were rarely produced with a theme in mind. Rather, the tapes were as disorganized as closets that failed to provide a friendly storage space for a personal collection of tie-dye shirts, parachute pants, and high-top shoes. But unlike messy eighties closets, homemade mixtapes held a meaningful place in the hearts of listeners. After all, each individual mixtape often contained an inordinately discombobulated array of genres, from new wave to euro dance to pop rock. And the welcome disorganization of eighties mixtapes remains supreme over today's digital ones, simply because of the painstaking work invested in capturing the conglomeration of mini musical masterpieces in the reverberating space of the bedroom or home den.

ON TELEPHONES

Smartphones were barely zygotes, not even in their beginning stages of infancy, in the eighties. All social calls were made via the push-button landline telephone or, at its most advanced, the cordless phone. Unlike today's smartphones, telephones in the eighties weren't built with caller ID capabilities. For eighties youth, this meant total and joyful anonymity. A boy could nervously punch the buttons on the telephone keypad to surreptitiously call his unwitting crush, eagerly listen to the sweet sound of her voice saying "Hello," and quickly hang up with a swarm of butterflies fluttering in his stomach. And this was perfectly acceptable, without the least bit of creepiness to ruin an interaction that would otherwise never have happened in the hallways outside the seventh-grade classroom. Nowadays, if an unknown caller makes a call and immediately hangs up, it's absolutely certain that zero romantic intentions are behind it. It's as obnoxious as a dreaded spam call, where the intent is likely criminal, and the malicious caller attempts to somehow make a clean getaway with your hard-earned two hundred dollars. Even when it comes to something as rudimentary as the telephone, the all-around innocence of the eighties is sorely missed.

ON ANSWERING MACHINES

Along with eighties landline telephones were eighties answering machines. Bulky, boxy, and complex to use, answering machines gave imaginative individuals in this decade a tremendous dose of unbridled fun. While some polite outgoing messages got straight to the point, others showcased an impressive level of creative flair. These greetings extended for an entire minute; even at such a length, it was a shorter wait time than calling a company today, remaining on hold, and reluctantly falling asleep upon listening to the dull hold music. Some amateur eighties singers took the karaoke route and unabashedly greeted callers with song, fully put to rock music and blazing sound effects, letting them know no one's at home and requesting them to leave a message. If you couldn't record a hilarious outgoing message yourself, there were plenty of tapes to buy for $14.95 that delivered equivalent results. And, inspired by the creativity of these fabulous prerecorded greetings, callers were equally determined to leave messages that rivaled the inventiveness of the greetings themselves. How successful these callers were in their attempts to come off as entertaining as the recipients was not the point—all that mattered was that eighties callers unloaded fun and creative effort even into the smallest of everyday endeavors.

ON HOMEWORK

In comparison to today's rapid acquisition of knowledge, answers to homework questions didn't come easily for students in the eighties. Unlike now, where answers are found instantly with a tap of the touchscreen or a click of the computer mouse, completing yesteryear's homework was a far more challenging and time-consuming feat. Research took eons. Locating the right answer to one homework question was akin to digging for hours through the Venetia mines of Africa with a pickax to uncover a single natural diamond encrusted within the kimberlites. Performing research for a school paper took equally incredible effort. Students used the resources available to them at the time: the library card catalog, the ones in use one hundred years ago that required the monumental task of deciphering the mystifying Dewey Decimal System, or the encyclopedia. Mining through the hundreds of cards stuffed tightly in a single row in the enormous card catalog box on stilts was horrifically slow and provided little hopes of stumbling upon the right answer in a jiffy. And if the cards in the card catalog were handwritten rather than typed, good golly, the painstaking research would extend another garish hour. When the daunting card catalog failed to provide a clue, students resorted to sifting through the twenty-two volume sets of encyclopedias, like they were panning for gold in Nevada's Eldorado Canyon, once bursting with the prized nuggets. Nowadays, like the encyclopedia, the Eldorado Canyon is a ghost town, seldom frequented and no longer resourceful. You see, students in the eighties worked extra hard to complete a never-ending stream of school assignments. But their impressive effort built character. So don't dismiss the intelligence and gumption of kids in this glittering decade. By simply graduating, they demonstrated that entire collections of precious diamonds and gold were stored in those wild heads of extravagantly hair-sprayed hair.

ON PERMS

Permanent waves, affectionately known as perms, combined with an unapologetic indulgence of hairspray, produced a wildly voluminous look for the youth of the eighties. These no-nonsense big hairstyles stood literally three feet high by three feet wide in most formal portrait pictures of the high schoolers who earned enough pocket change from a fast-food job to buy a gargantuan supply of hairspray and afford regular perms at the local salon. Now it wasn't only highschoolers who sought this extravagant look of zigzag locks that no other decade even dared to permit. Pouty-lipped actresses gracing the silver screen, charmingly handsome sitcom actors cajoling laughs, front men singing in popular rock bands, and weather reporters all sported the look with genuine zeal. Straight hair was a no-no. Hair had to possess the big, shocking look of sticking your finger into an electric socket just long enough to produce a sizzle. And somehow the big perm hair of the eighties lasted the entire decade before it was replaced with the dramatically flattened, toned-down versions of subsequent years. Eighties hair was unlike any other in the history of humankind and shall forever retain its rank as the most expensive and hazardous hairstyle to maintain for any reasonable duration of time.

ON FILM CAMERAS

The 110 film camera made shooting photographs accessible to millions of everyday folks, a number that multiplied by a hundredfold during the decade of material excess. Featuring an all-mechanical design that didn't require batteries, the camera was loaded with 110 mm film and functioned as well as any practical camera would. Users could conveniently hold onto its fold-out case like a handle and snap photos of erupting geysers at Yellowstone National Park, ten-year-olds blowing party horns at birthday parties, and the pet dog chasing its own tail. Considering all the commotion, photos tended to appear rather blurry. Crystal-clear picture perfection hadn't yet been invented for the masses. Nevertheless, the cameras captured memorable events with ease. While the 110 film camera was a snap to use, it took a lengthy two weeks for the photo lab inside the neighborhood grocer or drug store to develop the film. Eighties kids who were privileged to own a 110 film camera would drop their roll of film into the circular free-standing film-collection bin and wait in anticipation for it to be developed fourteen days later. This meant the photo lab technicians would have a look-see at each of the twenty-four exposures on the film cartridge. Excitedly strolling over to the photo lab to pick up the freshly developed roll of film from the clerk meant a casual conversation was likely. Desired or not, the clerk would gab for a half hour about your family vacation to Yellowstone or offer tried-and-true tips to stop Skippy from chasing his own tail. Lost in later decades, this unintended sort of fellowship imbued almost everything in the eighties.

ON POCKET PROTECTORS

Eighties students sometimes wore pocket protectors, the mini pieces of ink-resistant plastic that securely held half a dozen pens—because, of course, any middle schooler would need more than four or five pens during the course of an average school day. Somehow, the pocket protector came to symbolize students who focused intently on schoolwork to the detriment of cultivating highly skilled social interactions. Naturally, if you concentrated more on doing homework than chatting with the sixth grader seated next to you, you'd need a multitude of writing instruments—and the pocket protector was believed to deliver flawlessly.

Now, the individual who patented the protective device must have been slightly out of whack, since pens should never be stored vertically, but horizontally. Tucking half a dozen ballpoint pens vertically meant that the ink could flow away from the tips of the pens, leak out into the plastic, and, with one misstep, could stain an entire shirtfront. And weren't pocket protectors specifically designed to prevent this very predicament? Ink clogs were a hazard, too, since the tips of the pens rested at the bottom crease of the dusty, dirty pocket protector. Anyone with a good head on their shoulders would have shied away from the useless trend for these very reasons. But the eighties were a charmingly inexplicable decade—just look at the predominance of pocket protectors sported by the purported intellectuals of the era.

ON PORTABLE MUSIC PLAYERS

Two hundred million music lovers clamored to buy the portable cassette player, fondly known to contemporaries as the Walkman, for a cool hundred bucks during its pinnacle in the eighties. The technology gave both youth and adults of the decade an opportunity to listen to music whenever and wherever they expressly wished. For instance, eighties music fanatics bought the Walkman to be entertained while donning spandex and leg warmers at the height of the aerobics craze, while walking with a confident swagger down the long city block, or while politely tuning out the din of fellow subway passengers without giving away their true intention. The Walkman grew to be a cultural icon during this freedom-loving decade, simply because you could plug in a pair of foam-covered headphones, press play, and privately immerse yourself in the glorious sounds from eighties tapes while in public. Folks no longer tethered to the stereo celebrated their newfound freedom—a pivotal characteristic of the eighties. Portable music was a breath of fresh air to an entire generation who were out and about, being forced to listen to the humdrum of heavy traffic, the nasal yakking of gossipy gal pals, or the incessant caws of highly intelligent black crows as they scavenged for the finest roadside pickings. The introduction of portable music in its convenient hand-held format meant that personal music choices took precedence over all else. Like most technology, the Walkman has since evolved from its heyday, but portable music remains an inseparable thread in the loosely woven fabric of society. You can, in fact, buy today's version of the Walkman for a cool three grand. And that tidy sum speaks to the impressive might of the diminutive portable cassette player with strong roots established in no other decade than the scintillating eighties.

ON PAYING CASH FOR EVERYTHING

Since the dawn of civilization, the world has been ruled by all sorts of kings: some outright incompetent, others perceivably transformative. But one capable king ruled the eighties—and that was cash. When they had it, people would pay for everything with cash, from a buffet meal with the family at the all-you-can-eat steakhouse restaurant to a plush teddy bear with a rainbow on its belly for the niece's fifth birthday. Cash was the preferred method of payment, if not the only one. Whether you shopped at the local yard sale or the trusty auto shop, merchants happily accepted cash. Even middle schoolers paid for lunches of microwavable pizza, 2 percent milk, and strawberry ice cream with none other than dollar bills and a pocketful of change. Eighties consumers knew exactly where their money went—so none of them suffered a heart attack when the final bill came. These wise folks stayed within budget, since they literally watched their money leave their hands. In effect, eighties consumers spent less when they paid in cash—the only option in most places of business at the time. The once-upon-a-time king of the eighties has since lost its power over today's spenders. Diverse forms of payment, from bitcoin to debit cards to mobile wallets, have usurped the king's rightful territory, thereby complicating financial transactions and, in general, mystifying the average spender. None of this financial coup d'état nonsense was prevalent in the eighties. Consumers just spent what they had, knew exactly where it all went, and could cut back when planning to purchase a little something special later on. Even financially, times were simpler. With the enduring power of eighties hair-sprayed bangs, cash is one king that deserves to be reinstated to the throne.

ON JEAN JACKETS

Cowboys and miners weren't the only ones to pick up on the jean jacket movement. Jean jackets, like seven-layer dip and cheeseburger pie, were also staples in the lives of eighties youth. Ranging in style from distressed to dark washed to stone washed to air brushed, a style of jean jacket was available to practically anyone with or without a taste for refinement. Jean jackets proliferated within the casual wardrobes of pop stars, movie stars, self-defined punks, and, of course, cool kids of all ages. Despite being a trend that fell into mainstream fashion as recently as the eighties, the decade's jean jackets are already considered vintage.

How quickly society refers to anything as freshly out of the eighties to be vintage. Goodness gracious, by these harsh standards, it makes forty-year-olds seem like antiques. Nevertheless, jean jackets represent classic American style. Don't be fooled, however. Jean jackets are still in vogue four decades after the eighties denim craze, being fashionably worn today in the same oversize styles reminiscent of the materialistic era when most items of clothing adhered to some form of obscuring shapelessness or outright bagginess. And for the attractive camouflaging attributes of everyday wear, you can thank eighties popular fashion.

ON SUPERMODELS

The willowy eighties supermodels, from Christy Turlington to Linda Evangelista, were stunning renditions of the human form, with breezy personalities to match—the whole package wrapped up in a luxurious purple velvet bow. Sensible and shrewd, supermodels of the day could command ten thousand dollars just for waking up in the morning. The otherworldly beauty of the era's only supermodels was exceptional, with supermodels expressing effortless self-assuredness and grace. In stark contrast to the ethereal loveliness and easiness of the eighties, today's models push social agendas rather than convince you to buy diamond-encrusted evening gowns for three grand. In the eighties, if you had it, you flaunted it. If you didn't have it, that was okay; you just didn't pretend that you did. The authenticity of the eighties saturated the beauty and fashion industries, raising them to glorious heights. These days of disingenuity are no different than being tricked into buying counterfeit cosmetics, believing they're the real deal, then being unpleasantly surprised when they cause a horrific case of acne. Standards are nonexistent. Seems like everyone's sister and their aunt Hilda and their Yorkshire terrier mix, Flippy, claim to be working models, oftentimes competing for the same gig. And it's no surprise when Flippy outdoes everyone and books the job. Never again will a decade lay credible claim to the well-earned title of *supermodel*, as that era has long passed, gone down like a blazing comet against the darkened starry sky. All said, the exquisite natural beauty of the eighties will neither be repeated nor forgotten.

ON ROLLER RINKS

Every eighties kid was thrilled with an afternoon at the roller rink. Whether roller rinks were a part of birthday parties or school field trips, the excitement was equally monumental. Once you paid the quarter, were handed your six-pound roller skates, tied up the painfully long row of laces, and carefully stomped your way over the thin, cheap carpeting toward the shiny, circular hardwood rink, you'd skate the entire two hours with an irrepressible grin on your face. It was common knowledge that you could skate backward—a highly impressive and inspiring feat when it happened— but this turned out to be impossible for the average self-taught roller skater. But you didn't care whether you zoomed forward or backward, because roller skating in any direction gave you unstoppable freedom. You could stop, of course, with the massive stoppers attached like stale jumbo marshmallows to the front tips of each roller skate. A slight learning curve was required, however, when it came to skillfully stopping without your entire body dangerously lunging forward and toppling over. If you dared, you could roller skate at speeds Mom and Pop weren't even allowed to drive in the eighties. Fortunately, for young break-neck daredevils, the railing around the periphery of the roller rink was a savior. Crash as you might into the railing, you'd fall and still laugh. Dazzling lightshows and the blast of funky eighties music made skating at the rink an electrifying part of youth. Best of all, no training or special skills whatsoever were required. Popping up all over America during the eighties, roller rinks gave every kid a taste of pure freedom rolled up in an unforgettable good time. Grown-ups today still lace on their roller skates, albeit sporting an excessively long list of protective gear, like knee pads, elbow pads, wrist pads, and a helmet, in attempts to recapture the nostalgia of eighties roller skating, but it's clearly a different flavor altogether.

ON LEG WARMERS

A fashion disaster peaking in the eighties, leg warmers were worn by people of all fashion sensibilities, ages, and professions. The trend of wearing leg warmers, even though you couldn't pirouette in any sense of the word, was thought to have originated inside dance studios, where dancers attempted to keep their calves warm and prevent cramping. Due to popular movies, leg warmers took off in the general population like oven mitts in a commercial bakery. Everyone wanted them and weren't afraid to wear them over everything, from jeans to tights to leggings. Clearly, the insatiable desire to stay warm predisposed

41

an entire decade. Internationally acclaimed pop singers sported leg warmers and tights as if they were preparing to hit the aerobics floor rather than perform on the music stage in front of wild audiences numbering in the thousands. Leg warmers were stylishly and smartly worn over fancy three-inch heels during nights out, because it was absolutely critical you kept your calves from cramping during a four-course dinner with a handsome gentleman on date night at the swanky seafood restaurant downtown. Youths even wore them over roller skates, thoughtfully making a combined style-and-safety statement. After all, a quality pair of leg warmers could prevent a nasty scrape from a tumble on the hard surface of the roller rink. It didn't matter if it was blistering cold or a scorching one hundred degrees outside—leg warmers found their way onto the calves of even the most practical folks. No matter what drove the questionable trend of wearing leg warmers over every possible piece of feminine attire, like most curious things from the eighties, the fashion mishap is today making a gradual and surprisingly courageous comeback.

ON BIGNESS

Everything grew noticeably enormous in the eighties, from manes of hair sprayed to stand several inches high to parachute pants designed to appear oddly wide in strategically confusing places. While big hair and big clothes were big deals, restaurant food portions, too, were bigger in comparison to decades prior. A double-stacked hamburger, made into a satisfying meal with the inclusion of a paper bag of crisp fries and a large soda, was a whopping amount of food for an average eighties American to wolf down. It's no wonder that body sizes also grew proportionally— bigger. In contrast to today, however, that hamburger meal has shrunk in size, meaning fast-food diners in the eighties got the biggest bang for their buck. Fast-food drink sizes grew to mammoth proportions during the eighties, starting with a meager thirty-two ounces at the turn of the decade, then impressively doubling by the end of it. And the behemoth size of sodas still hadn't finished its growth phase. These days, bags of potato chips have been steadily and surreptitiously getting smaller, despite manufacturers secretly praying no one will notice, making the number of ounces of crisps in the eighties significantly larger. And it doesn't stop with food. Shampoo bottles have since gotten smaller, which is, thankfully, timely, since folks in the eighties needed all the shampoo they could muster out of the bottle to wash out the sticky residue of those massive gobs of hairspray.

ON GLOBAL WARMING

While global warming was a growing problem as far back as the eighties, it wasn't the tragic debacle it is today. In the eighties, the East Antarctic glacier was actually an immense, frozen, and profoundly breathtaking natural splendor, unlike now, where the ice is melting at a swift rate of seventy billion tons a year. Ocean currents were faster once upon a time. But because of the rapid, ice-cold glacial melt entering the warm ocean water, today's currents are slowing considerably. While Antarctica's vanishing glaciers may be an afterthought for some, global warming is affecting ordinary people in everyday life.

Old Man Winter boasted robust health in the eighties. Now, he's declined to a noticeably feeble condition and on the verge of needing around-the-clock hospice. When Old Man Winter commanded the season with full-bodied strength, you could speed down a steep hill in a red plastic winter sled in the backyard of the local library, because the fluffy snowfall had accumulated to an impressive eight to ten inches. Today's snowfall is comparably paltry. Precipitation might fall, but due to global warming, it's mostly in the form of raindrops. In the eighties, long, clear icicles prettied up the leafless tree branches outside your kitchen window and the rooftops of every neighbor's house each winter. You could build snowmen and feel confident that these winter companions would share their rapture for the season for at least a month, albeit smiling awkwardly through their three-button mouth. But today's skimpy snowmen, if Old Man Winter permits them to be built at all, might survive a pathetic day or two before melting into oblivion. Moreover, eighties kids expected a white Christmas every December—and got it.

ON CARTOONS

L ife was simpler back in the day. Cartoons, ranging from the traditional cat-and-mouse chase in *Tom and Jerry* to the health-conscious sailor in *Popeye* gulping spinach without realizing it contained all the B vitamins necessary for the strong heart and lung capacity to fight off the bad guy, reflected that simplicity. The classical music that accompanied the hand-drawn animation frames introduced eight-year-olds to the magnificent composers of the eighteenth and nineteenth centuries like no elite university education today ever could. Eighties cartoons, by all standards, were the embodiment of capricious fun and classiness—just what a kid growing up in this decade needed as a foundation for living out a well-balanced life. In stark contrast, today's overwhelming multitude of diverse computer-animated cartoons push social or moral agendas and fail to hold up to the innocent slapstick humor reminiscent of this beloved and long-missed decade. Eighties cartoons kept kids wholesomely entertained for hours without indoctrinating them into some complex social or moral ideal. "Good guy versus bad guy" was the primary theme behind eighties cartoons, and how effective it was! Young audiences learned that stealing a juicy carrot from the wily farmer would only end poorly—hilariously, but still poorly. Let it be said, reverting back to the simplicity of the good old days is sometimes preferable.

ON BEING A LESS LITIGIOUS DECADE

L awsuits have had the purpose of bringing justice to mistreated individuals since the emergence of the legal system in 1789. But nearly two hundred years later, not as many folks pursued the expensive legal route for every perceived wrongdoing. In the eighties, it was unheard of to file lawsuits because of high school grades missing a plus sign or ugly babies suggesting unfaithfulness in the marriage or the dry cleaner accidentally losing a pair of men's pastel slacks. Sure, in the eighties, weather reports were issued during the course of the news hour. Sometimes the meteorologist predicted sunshine instead of rain. But no one ever considered filing a lawsuit because the weather report was off by a torrential rain shower or two, causing an individual's carefully made plans to be completely bungled. In the decade before the prolific spread of coffee shops, people never sued when their cup of iced coffee contained a little too many ice cubes, thereby decreasing the volume of their cool caffeinated drink by an infinitesimal amount. During the eighties, restaurants could sell chicken sandwiches without fearing they'd be sued in the event they ran out of stock of the fried bird and the buns to go with it. Beer companies could run ads showing how beer might introduce spirited, bikini-clad women into the lives of television audiences without risking being sued for failing to deliver and contributing to a viewer's emotional distress and financial loss. In the relaxed, sensible, bygone decade of the eighties, the United States simply hadn't yet earned notoriety for being among the most litigious societies in the world.

ON THE BIRTH OF TWENTY-FOUR-HOUR NEWS

News mania was not a phrase you'd hear thrown around before the eighties. No one was that fascinated with the news to want to watch it every hour of every day of every year. Who was the sadistic media entrepreneur who invented twenty-four-hour news, anyway, exposing every level of society nonstop to the worst of the world? Was life really as terrifying as the news unhesitatingly reported for a straight twenty-four hours? All-day news convinced every stable household that it was so. Sensationalism spun the same stories into dramatically different ones, with all of them airing as new stories on each television station. You had to keep eighties audiences at the edge of their seats, and you couldn't accomplish that by airing the same old stories day in and day out. News reporters expertly hid their abhorrence of the endless repetition—either that, or they lacked a beating human heart. Before the turn of the decade, audiences tuned in to watch the news once or twice per day, when it aired. It was a well-adjusted relationship: news aired, and audiences watched. Reminders of the possibilities and the realities of world catastrophes were not shoved in your face like a whipped cream pie by the red-nosed birthday party clown. Ha-ha! *Balanced* defined the era of news prior to the eighties. But when all-day news started to air at the start of the decade, that sense of peaceful equilibrium vanished in an instant. You could grow jittery by binge-watching twenty-four-hour news, needing ongoing therapy to return any semblance of normalcy to your life. The alternative was just to turn off the news in favor of watching something less threatening to your entire existence and more entertaining, like those oddball characters in *Cheers* who showed up at the bar every evening to sit, drink, and share their woes or triumphs, resulting in a hilarious half hour of eighties television sitcom bliss.

ON PEACE

A feeling of peace wove through the lives of eighties youth like soft threads through a Sunbonnet Sue Amish quilt. Terrorists were only a figment of the imagination, making more appearances on fictional television shows than in real life. You'd hear about less than a handful of terrorist activities that disrupted life in some far away nation, never quite hitting US soil and causing massive upheaval. For the large part, in the eighties the beloved country remained safe from the grips of international terrorism. While the world stage received violent blows every now and then from earth-shaking terrorist plots, the home front remained protected like the Castle of the Moors on the Iberian Peninsula in the ninth century. Similarly, during the mostly peaceful years of the eighties, gun violence was not the unfortunately massive and spontaneous threat it is today. At most, eighties youth shot water guns, drenching every nearby friend and having an innocent sort of blast. Kids never feared getting wounded by stray bullets as they rode their bikes around the neighborhood, flipped through a picture book in the living room, or stood at the bus stop each morning. Six-year-olds didn't carry weapons to school and show them off to wide-eyed peers during afternoons of show-and-tell. In fact, everyday peace was such a common expectation in the eighties that no student needed to find the courage and full-body armor just to attend class a walkable distance from home. Peace was familiar to all of eighties youth, just as the famous tie-dyed peace sign was, and fully savored in its moment.

ON OPTIMISM FOR THE FUTURE

The world was smaller, more tightly knit, and friendlier during the incomparable eighties. Hope for the future gushed through everyone's veins, from junior high kids excited to be growing up to high schoolers just graduating and confidently handling their new responsibilities in the real world. In the span of these ten years, people genuinely cared, whether they were the mustached, bodybuilding school principal chatting with students in his button-down shirt and savvy suspenders or the petite hospital nurse discussing the joys of her interracial marriage. Growing up in the eighties meant you believed the existing problems of the world were inching closer toward positive resolutions, and that mistakes of past decades were being corrected, thereby serving to benefit current and future eras. The eighties contrasted starkly with the present day, where both televised and online news sources maliciously convince you that fearsome dangers lurk everywhere, and blamefully insinuating that the average person fails to do her part to improve matters. Instead, the eighties were a carefree, unmatched, and fervently missed decade that will never again be seen or enjoyed except in long-term memory. Nevertheless, for the optimistic, the heights of the eighties' unsurpassed glory will remain forever cherished in the hearts and minds of folks who grew up in the best decade of their lives.

Thank you for reading *In Defense of the Eighties*.
If you enjoyed this fling with the eighties,
please consider leaving a review at your favorite retailer,
and help others discover books of retro humor.

Books in the In Defense Of series
In Defense of the Grim Reaper
In Defense of Seniorhood
In Defense of Misfortune
In Defense of Cupid
In Defense of Animalhood

Visit my author website
www.riyapresents.com

9 781956 496130